What Ca

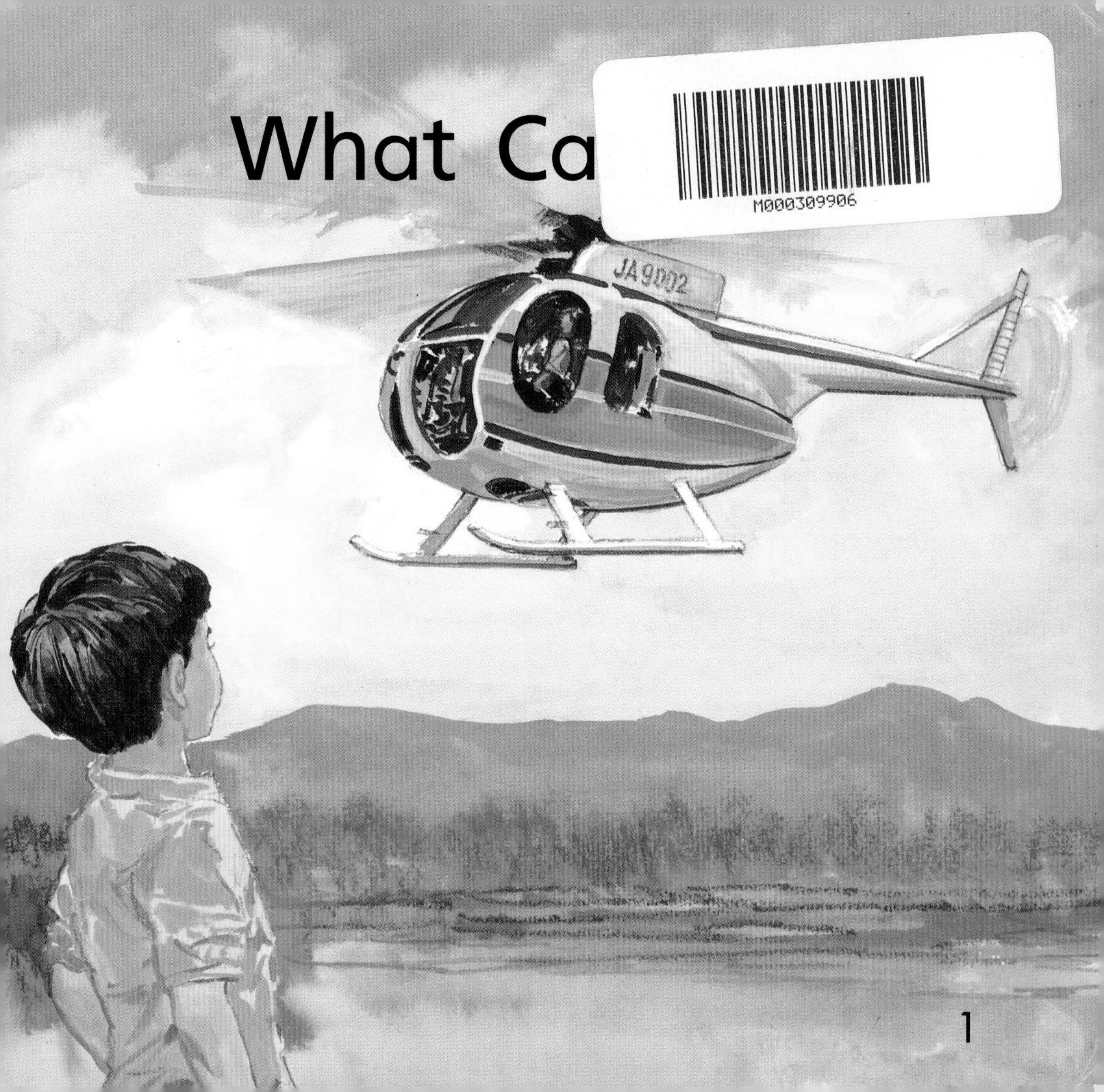

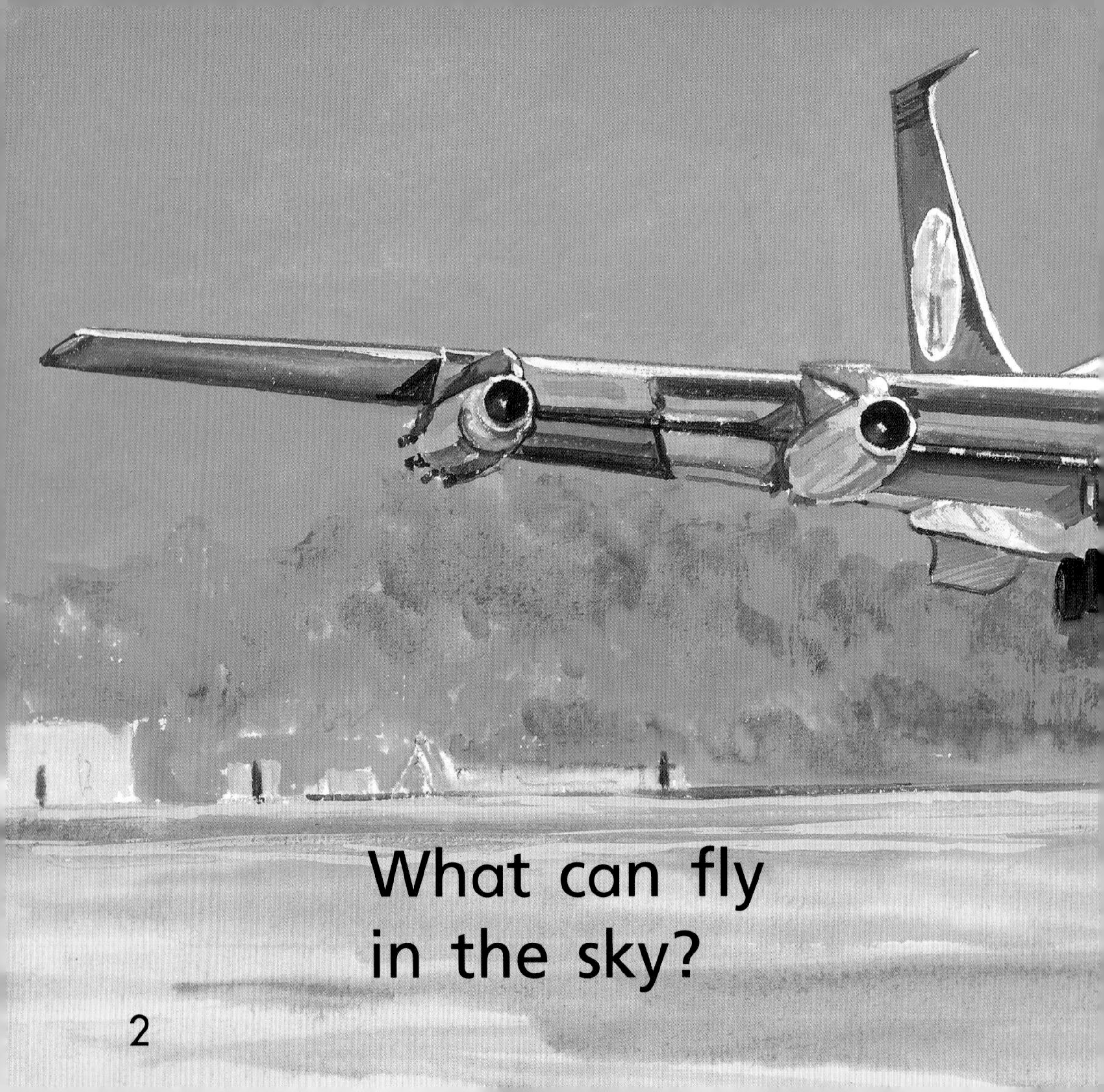

What can fly
in the sky?

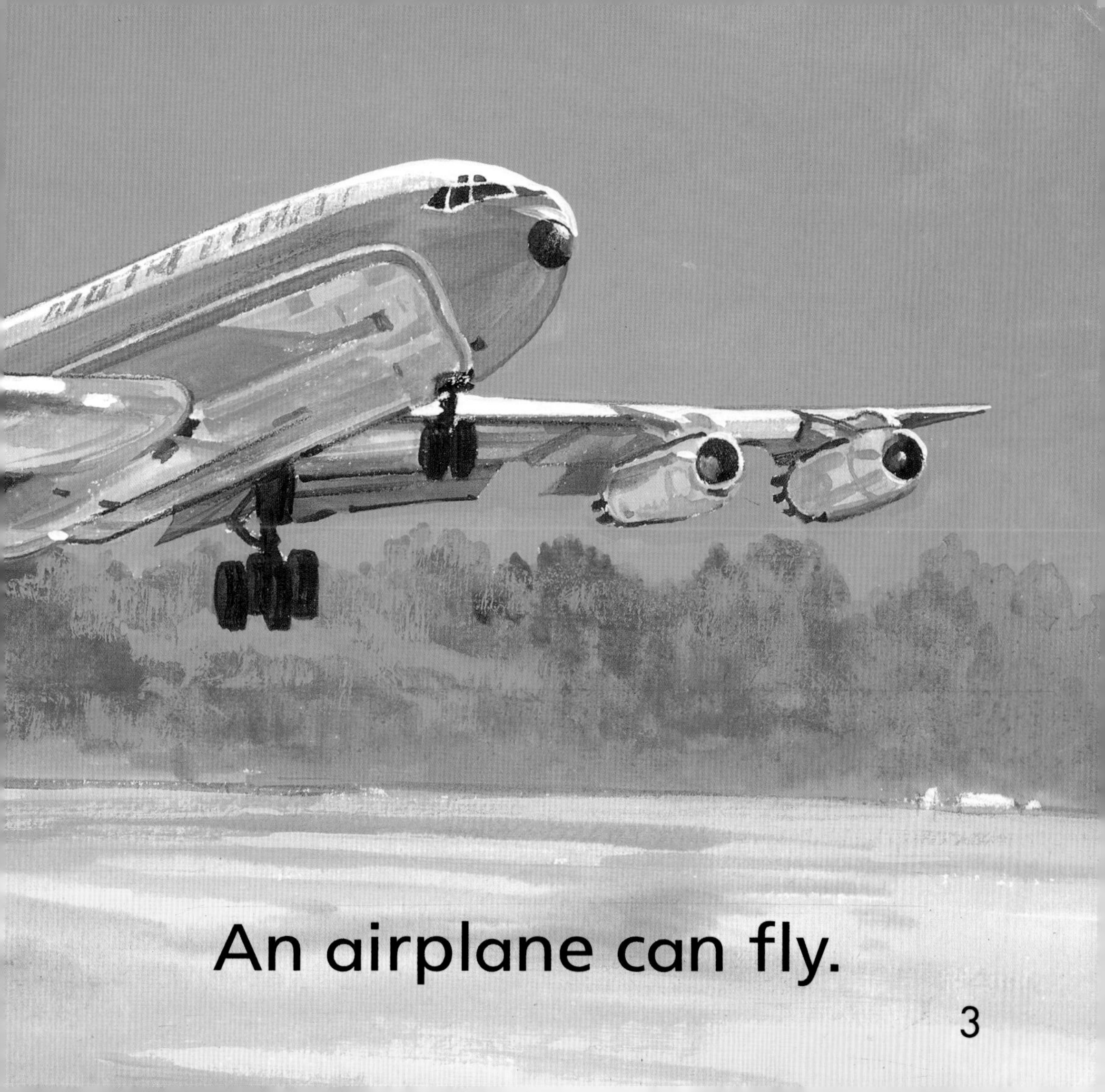

An airplane can fly.

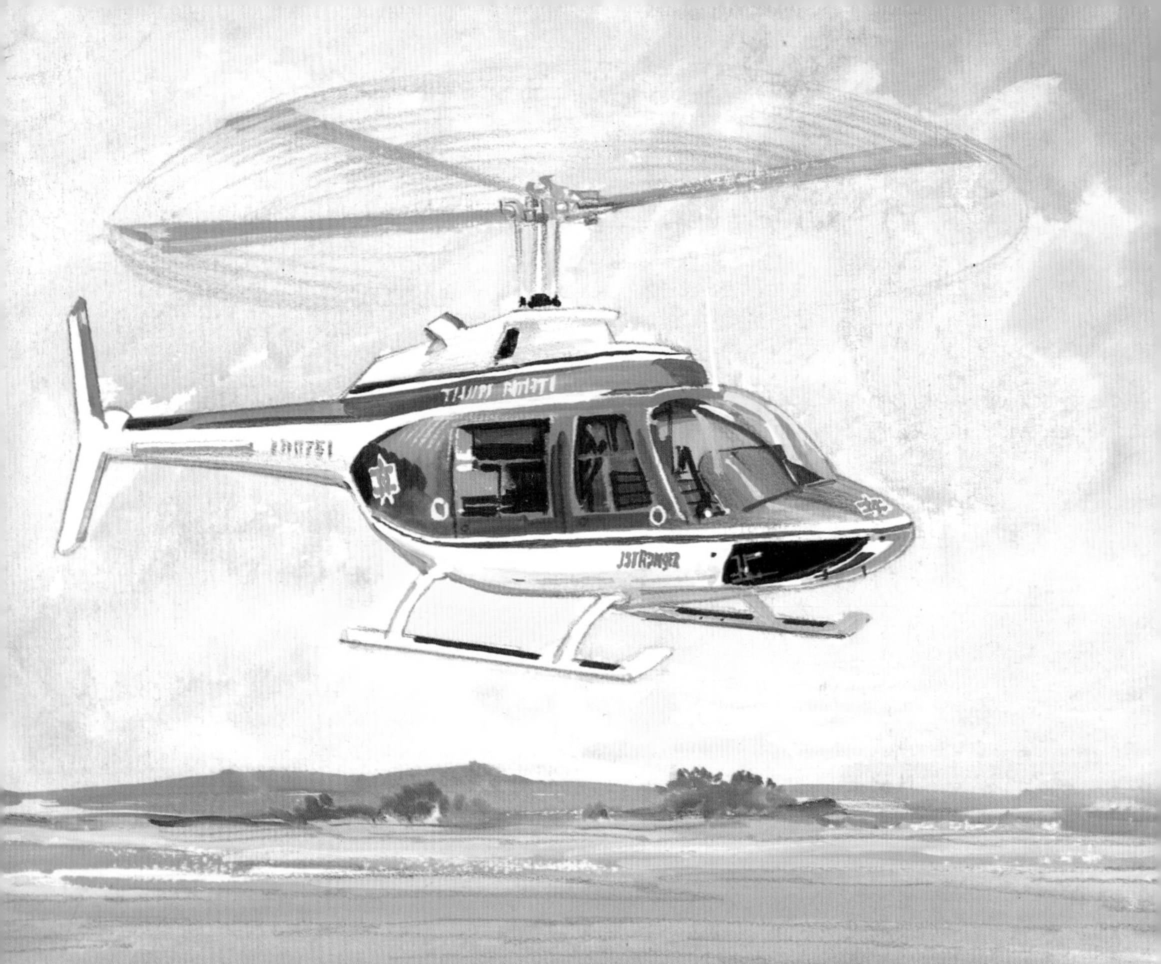

A helicopter can fly.

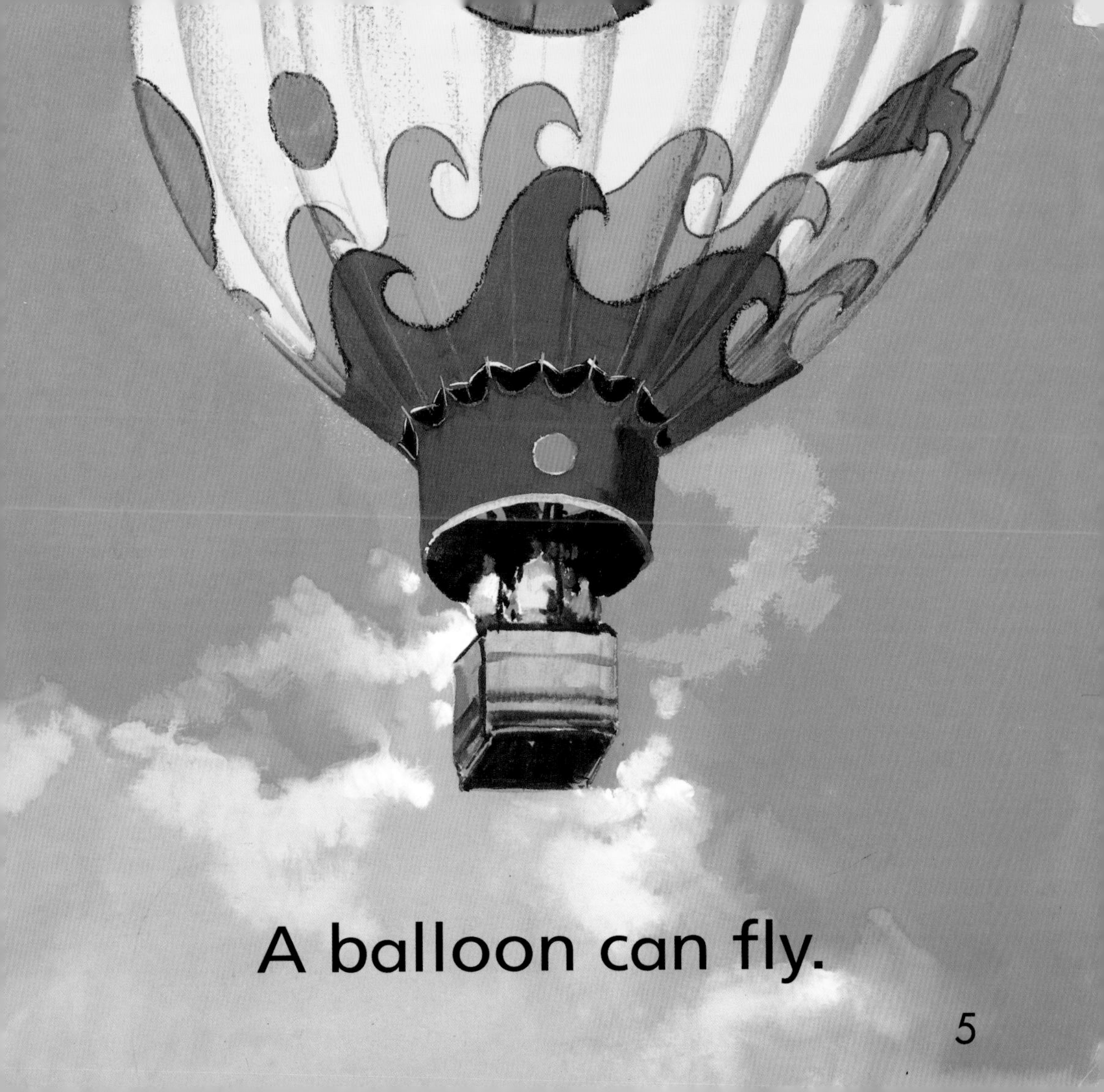

A balloon can fly.

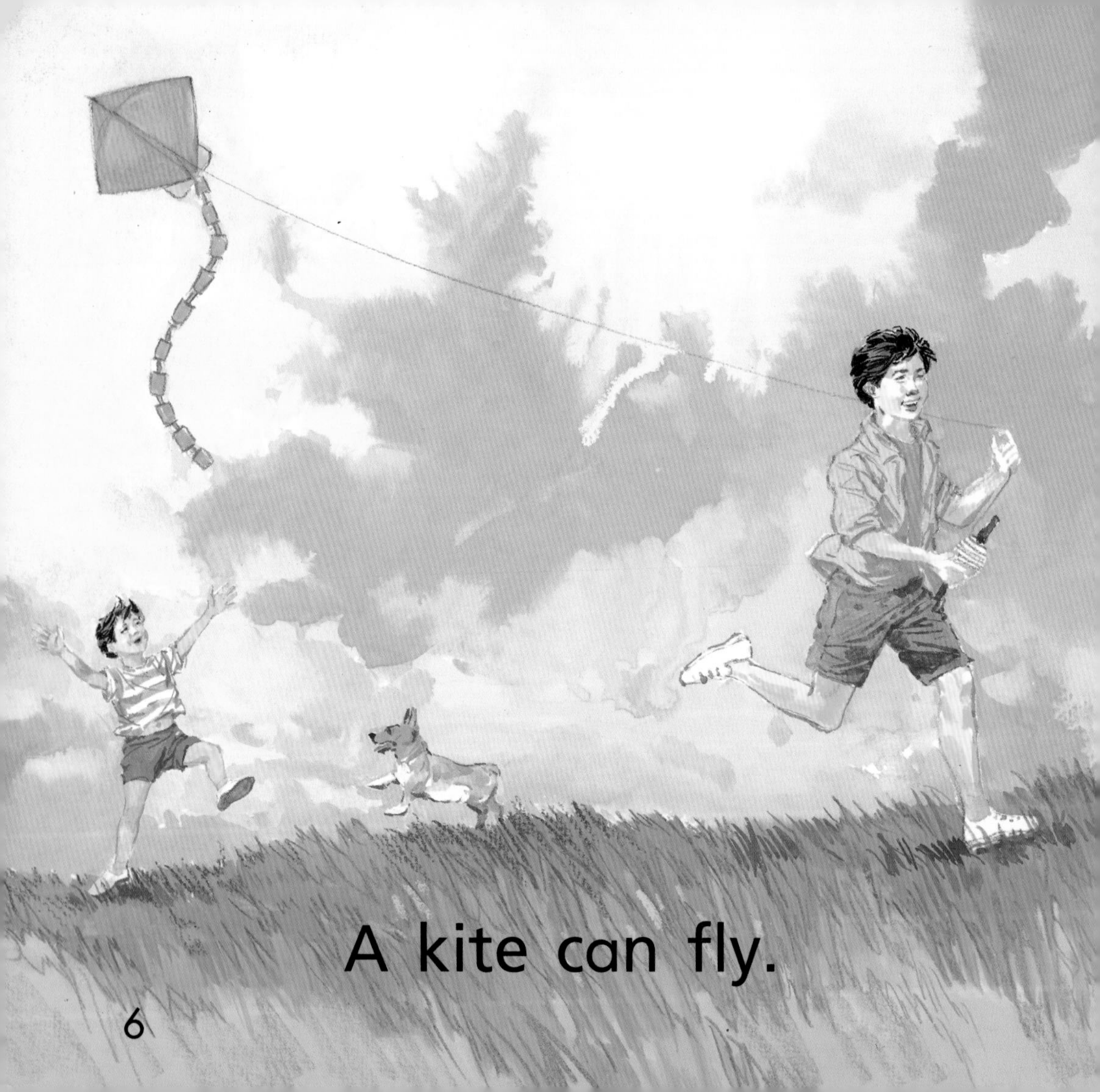

A kite can fly.

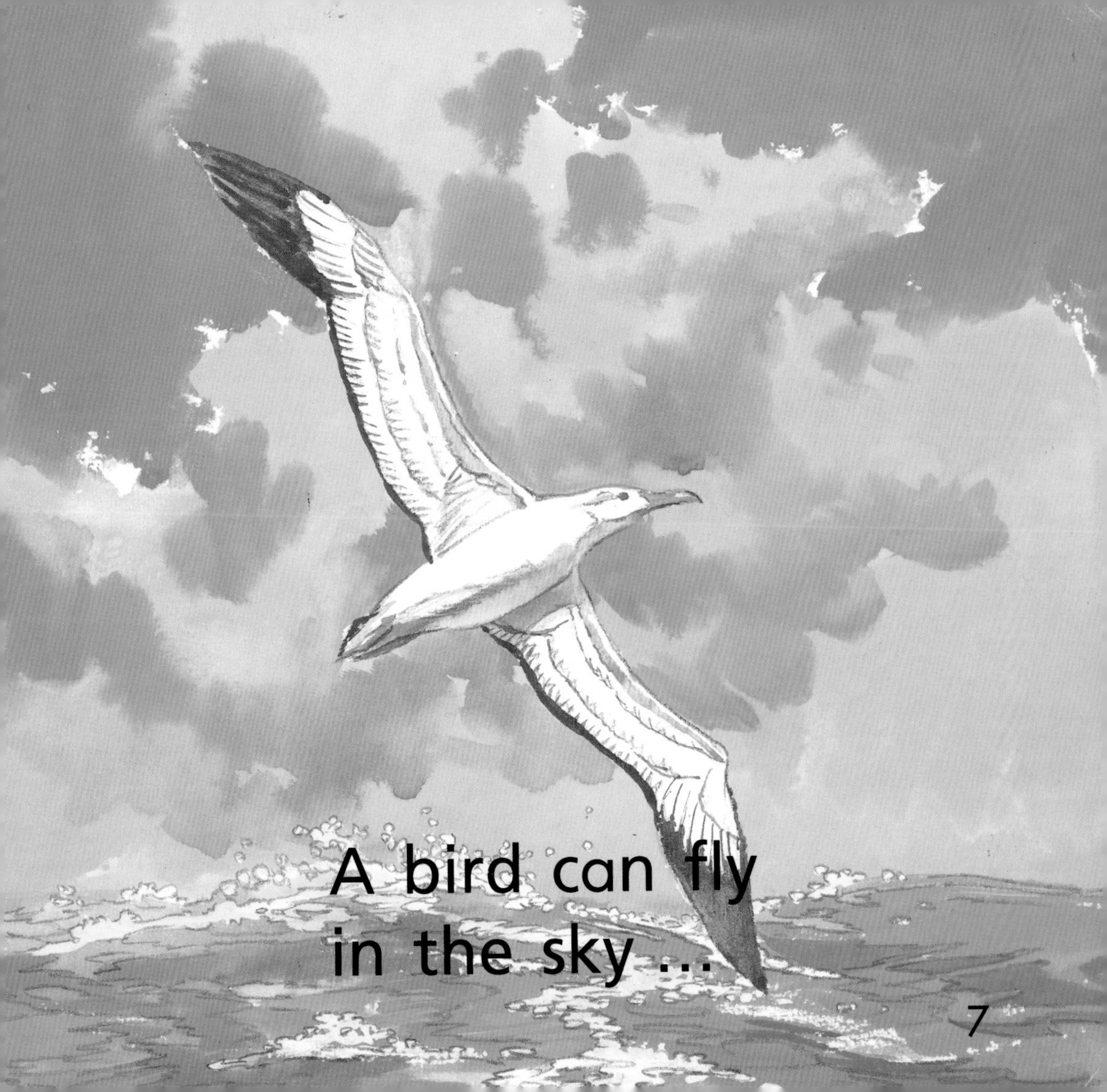

A bird can fly
in the sky ...

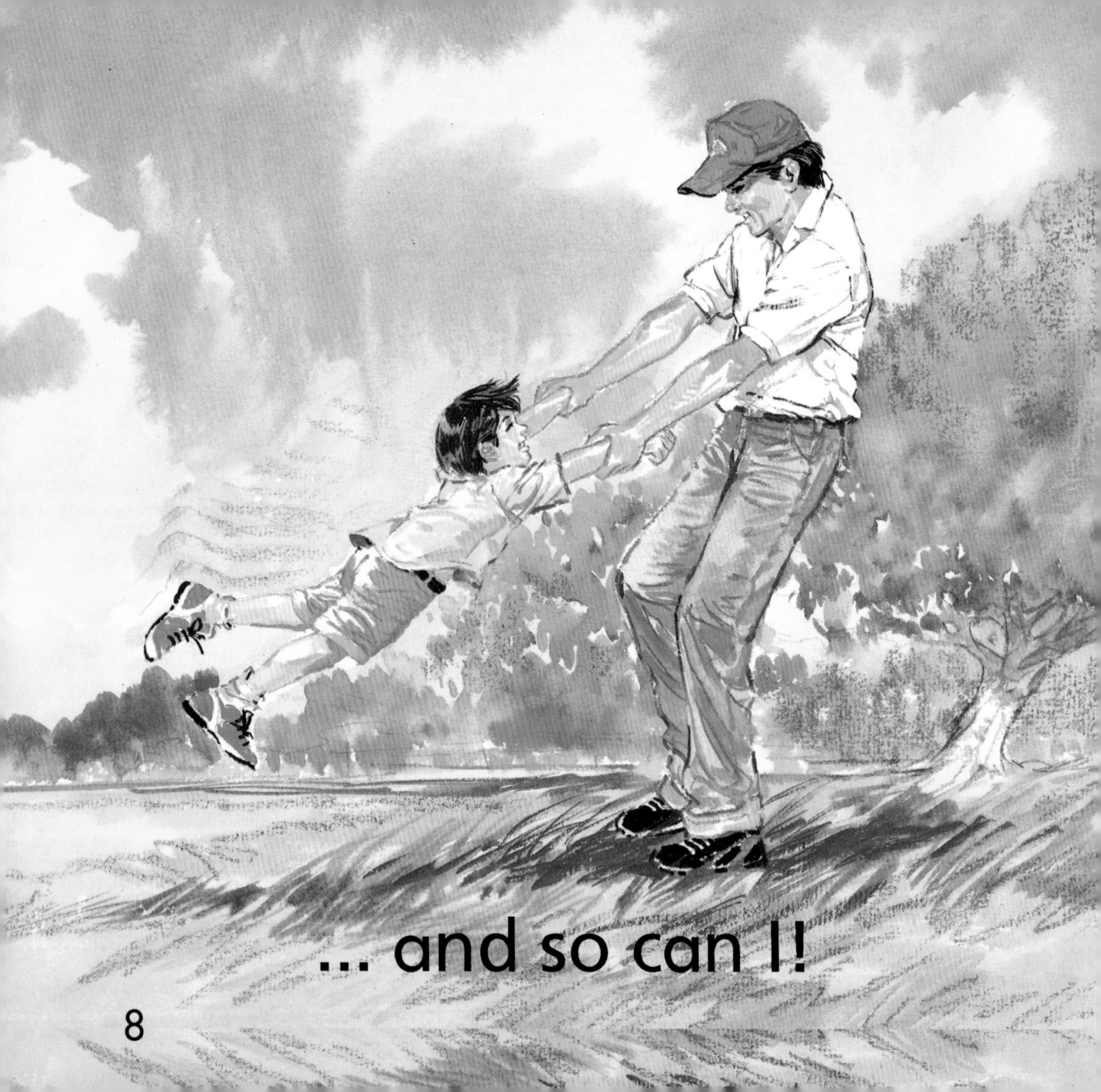

... and so can I!